METAL DETECTING BEGINNERS TO PRO GUIDE

(2020 Edition)

A Quick beginners Guide to pin pointing Hidden Treasures at Beaches, underwater and the right digging tools to get started

FREDRICK
COBLE

Copyright

Contents

Chapter One

Introduction

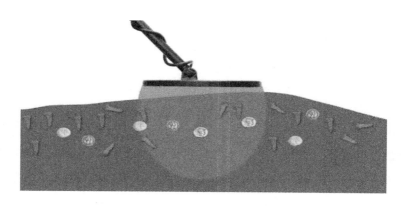

The use of metal detectors to find treasure is something quite recent thanks to improved technologies. Our ancestors prospected for gold or precious metals using picks, stoves, and then a rattle. Although the pan and pan are the traditional tools for prospecting that have the best price/performance ratio, technological develop- ments offer the treasure miner a wide range of possibilities. It is now possible to use a metal detector. This alternative is especially intended for those who are looking for something new and a fun way to find treasure.

If you walk on the seaside beaches early in the morning before they are taken over by tourists, you should see people accompanied by their beach finder pacing up and down the beach. Some people live exclusively from finding and selling gold lost by others. On tourist beaches, you can find rings, bracelets, necklaces, earrings, or watches that have lost their owner and have fled into the sand. But metal detectors aren't just for that. They can also allow you to find gold nuggets and become real treasure hunters like those of the Thames presented in this magnificent report from National Geography.

History of Archeology and Metal Detectors

With the rise and development of scientific and technological archeology, since the early 1950s, shallow methods of geophysical detection and others have been introduced to archaeological exploration, and gradually formed a geophysical prospecting. The most commonly used methods are the resistivity method, the electromagnetic method, and the ground-penetrating radar method. As a specific application of the electromagnetic method, the metal detector is an instrument specially used to detect metal. Because of archaeological excavations, there is a considerable number of antique metal products. For example, gold, silver, coins, bronze, and other precious metals on behalf of cultural wealth and power. Therefore, the metal detector has gradually become an important exploration tool of archaeologists. In recent years, the rise in the West "hot treasure hunt" to further accelerate metal detectors, underground metal detectors, and research in the field of archeology, production, and promotion.

The superiority of metal detectors in archeology

Is compared to many conventional archaeological exploration methods. The metal detector, having precise positioning, simply and effectively detects a large degree of resolution and strong advantages. Its superior performance mainly results in three aspects: the target positioning function, the target sounding function, and the target screening function. Before digging the target, you must first determine the exact location of the target. This is generally after the end of a wide range of geophysical prospecting using a beginner metal detector to detect a mesh in the target area found. It also depends on the size of the acoustic signal to gradually reduce the range of the measured object, until the high-frequency acoustic signals are emitted. Combined with the polling and filtering functions, you can precisely extract valuable targets. It should be noted that the electromagnetic field generated by the metal detector is affected by the eddy currents formed on the surface of the metal body. For the same metallic body, the intensity of the acoustic signal produced by it is only positively linked to the surface and is not linked to its mass.

Some metal detectors indicate the depth indicated on the scale values. It also indicates when there is a particular target and can indicate the target table substantially indicating the depth. Its basic principle is: with a fixed metal body as a reference, refer to the indication of the head caused by the metal body at different depths and delimit different values of indication of the depth. Such metal detectors are more suitable for finding metallic objects having similar shapes, such as metal coins, bullets, and the like.

In the past, detection using detectors was weak and the detection of minerals in the soil also produced an audible signal, misleading the results of the detection. This phenomenon of soil mineralization is called "mineralization reaction". For this reason, the old detectors are powerless in places with complex geological structures. Nowadays, the underground metal detector has not only excluded the influence of the "mineralization reaction", but can also distinguish the value of the object measured according to the sound signal emitted by the instrument when the target is detected.

The term "public archeology" was first proposed by the American archaeologist Charles McGimsey in "Public Archeology" published in 1972. Tens of thousands of archaeological remains have been discovered each year, the most famous being Terry Herbert, who used detectors to find 1,500 treasures on a farm in Staffordshire, England. To promote interaction between the public, metal detectors, archaeologists, and museums, 199 metal detection clubs participate in 927 meetings organized by the club. The mobile cultural relics program has greatly stimulated public interest and enthusiasm for archeology: thanks to metal detectors, the public can also make an important contribution to archeology and history.

Finding treasures with a Metal Detector

You see, unlike many other objects created in history, there are pieces of metal. This gives them a higher probability over time and today. Ancient coins of bronze, gold, silver, and other metals can be found today using metal detectors. These modern machines can help amateurs and researchers to detect stratification and find these precious and historically important objects. Also, if ancient coins are found in an area, the entire area can be carefully excavated by archaeologists, and many other historical finds can be found.

Ancient treasures offer a unique view of history. Many people have been ruined by rulers, warriors, temple walls, and even everyday images. If we look at the coins in our pockets, in archaeological terms, like the old coins, the visual details of these coins allow people to better understand the culture of possession of money. Without this story, most information may not be passed onto future generations.

Given the social type of coins used in history, one of the best places to find deposits of ancient coins in Europe. Recently, two beginner metal detector enthusiasts from the island of Jersey Strait in northern Europe discovered more than 50,000 pieces of copper dating from 50 BC. Rich returned to the Human Rights Commission. It was discovered that these Celtic coins were just a huge plot after discovering around 60 silver coins and a gold coin a few months ago. If they cannot find these old coins, these parts of the past may have been lost for future generations.

However, even with the coin validator, finding the old coins and treasures is not easy, the above person has searched the same area for 30 years before discovering the cache of this ancient coin! However, having the best coin detectors will help because old coins are sometimes located in treasure chests or underground treasure chests. Two metal detectors can be used to find these larger treasures.

To find treasures with a metal detector a few steps must be followed.

1. Choose the right metal detector according to your budget:

There are all prices with very different performances. You must set a target for harvested gold and based on this target see how much you are ready to invest to get there. Although the price is not always a guarantee of quality, it nevertheless appears that the so-called more professional models are the most suitable for finding gold nuggets. By buying this type of tool, it is more likely that you will find good gold nuggets, which can be resold at a good price and thus return the investment of your metal detector quickly.

2. Tame your equipment

How a metal detector works

Metal detectors have two coils. The first, emitting, becomes an electromagnet when it is energized. This electromagnet will create a magnetic field around it. When this field meets a metal, it will in turn produce a magnetic field that will "bounce" against the metal detector and be detected by the receiving coil. This phenomenon will be coupled with a sound that will sound when metals are present. Nowadays, a good number of metal detectors are made for a specific purpose, the jewelry detector will be more adapted to the search for jewelry, the gold detector will be intended for the search for gold nuggets.

Concentric search and Extended search

There are two types of coils, the concentric ones which allow locating metals in the ground under the ground. Wide search coils are more effective for finding and prospecting for surface metals. They cover larger areas of research, however, they are less suitable for in-depth research.

Accessories to take with you

With your metal detector you will also need some accessories which may prove useful:

- Headphones for better, clearer sound.
- A cloth to clean your metal detector.
- And as with all your forwarding expeditions:
- A shovel and a claw tool to dig up metals
- Tubes or other glass jars to store your finds.
- detector and shovel

3. Your first steps with your equipment

Read the instructions for your detector carefully. Familiarize yourself with its features and accessories. Practice in your garden with a little gold to check that the device is working properly.

Chapter Two

Metal Detectors

Types of Metal Detectors

The first detectors worked according to the frequency beat principle but they were not very efficient. The technique of very low frequencies gave better sensitivity, but in the 1960s, pulse induction was developed and is still the most used today.

Frequency beat

Frequency beat detectors were the first to appear because they are simple to implement but they are also the least sensitive. The principle is the frequency beat. It uses two oscillators, one fixed, the other sensitive to changes in the magnetic field. The modification of the magnetic field of the coil influences, as we have seen, on its inductance and therefore, if an oscillator is built around it, it will have a frequency that reacts with the magnetic field and therefore the presence of metal.

To use it, simply compare the signal from this oscillator with a reference signal; the latter represents the signal of the first oscillator which would not be modified by the presence of metal. The compared signal can be used to light a diode or be connected to an amplifier to hear via a loudspeaker the difference in frequencies if it is between 20Hz and 30kHz.

Very low frequency

The frequencies used are less than 20kHz. This detector is made up of two coils, a transmitter, and a receiver. The transmitting coil crossed by a sinusoidal current generates around it a magnetic field; when a metallic object passes through this magnetic field, eddy currents appear within it. These currents in turn generate a magnetic field that tends to compensate for the magnetic field created by the emitting coil. The receiving coil will react to the magnetic field emitted by the metal object, an induced current will pass through it. This current process by the electronics makes it possible to know whether or not there is a metallic object.

This detector makes it possible to discriminate between metals and Ferro magnetics. The signal perceived by the take-up reel is out of phase with the transmitted signal. The phase shift depends on the metals and thus makes it possible to discriminate them. For a prospector, the goal is to get rid of small iron objects above all. Discriminating aluminum runs the risk of missing interesting alloy targets such as the log, the electrum, the gossip (which have been used throughout the ages to make coins), and even gold.

The frequency of the oscillator on which the detector operates determines its quality of response to precious metals as well as its resistance to ground effects. Thus the higher its frequency (above 10kHz and very beyond, around 20kHz) the more it will be sensitive to scrap metal and soil disturbances, and the less it will feel precious metals. Below 10 kHz or even lower, the devices become insensitive to ground effects reducing their performance

Pulsed induction

The pulsed induction detector requires only one coil. These detectors are very efficient in deep research. They can detect up to 1.50 m below the ground for small objects and up to around 3.50 m for large metallic masses. A powerful current pulse is sent into the coil. Each pulse generates a very brief magnetic field. When the pulse ends, the polarity of the field reverses and suddenly collapses which causes a current peak, the return pulse.

This lasts a few microseconds and causes another current through the coil. The process repeats. If the detector is above a metallic object, the pulse creates an opposite magnetic field in the object. When the pulse stops, the magnetic field of the object increases the duration of the return pulse. A test circuit makes it possible to check the duration of the return pulse. By comparing it with the start length, the circuit determines whether another magnetic field has extended the decay time of the return pulse.

These detectors do not necessarily have the oval plate shape of conventional low-frequency detectors. There are some in the form of a 1 × 1 m or 2 × 2 m frame, to be lifted with both hands, these then only detect masses the size of a fist, so not the small parts. But there are smaller frames, close to the size of a conventional tray, which detects parts and other small objects, still using pulse induction technology. This type of detector is also found in the form of two small frames connected by a bar that attaches to a conventional detector dashboard. Their performance in discrimination is much less important than those at low frequency. On the other hand, they are much less sensitive to soil effects. The first models were static (moving from one detection zone to another then remaining static for detection), we now find semi-static ones where we can move very slowly in the field.

Uses of Metal Detectors

Demining

The aim of military demining is to allow units to make their way through a minefield or to secure a military environment (camp, base) where mines have been hidden, humanitarian demining which tends to return mined land accessible, safe for surrounding populations.

Archeology

Metal detectors are sometimes used professionally in the field of archeology. Indeed, the fundamental objective of this one is not the collection of metallic objects but their update within the framework of methodical excavations like the programmed excavation, by documenting the context with which they were associated. Metal detectors are therefore used marginally for verification purposes or in emergency contexts as part of a preventive search.

Also, metal detectors are subject to uncontrolled use or "treasure hunts", which may conflict with the preservation of heritage and considered to be clandestine excavation. For the Happah association which fights against the looting of archaeological heritage, "Leisure metal prospecting often has catastrophic repercussions on the integrity of archaeological sites. Most recreational detection practitioners, the "detectors" (tens of thousands) do not have prospecting permits. Only a few dozen people have it in France. Consequently, very many archaeological objects (several thousand if currencies, fibulae, etc. are taken into account) are not declared to the SRA and are not published. It is therefore a gigantic loss of information which is nevertheless crucial for science. Historical and archaeological sites are then deprived of part of the potential information that they could have delivered in the case of a systematic prospecting (metallic artifacts). "Different legislative responses have been made to these threats depending on the country.

Metal Detector Brands

If you are starting to develop a passion for metal detection and soil prospecting, or you want to spend your time outdoors looking for little treasures, relics, ancient coins, and gold nuggets. It is therefore high time to put the little dishes in the big ones and invest in a good metal detector But which one to choose and which are the most interesting brands on the market?

It's not easy to make a choice when you're in the initiation period! We give you a tip: if you are a beginner, and you want a quality metal detector while being affordable and easy to use, a manufacturer imposes himself, he comes from Texas and his name is Garrett. You can also opt for the Deus brand if you want to go a little further.

Metal detectors from Garrett, an illustrious Texan manufacturer

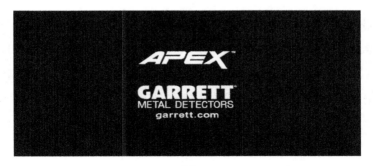

Garrett is an American brand of metal detectors founded by a visionary: Charles Garrett. This guy has revolutionized the world of metal detection and soil prospecting with his innovations and the great technological advances of his metal detectors intended for the general public. Garrett is responsible in many ways for the popularization of the concept and the introduction of this hobby in families passionate about the outdoors.

Charles Garrett, a Navy officer who notably worked on the technology planted on the moon by a certain Neil Armstrong, began to design and manufacture metal detectors in his garage in 1963. In 1964, he embarked on the business with his wife Eleanor. The tandem wasted no time in launching the Hunter Hunter double coil, which would, therefore, be their first metal detector intended for the public.

Business flourished at Garrett Metal Detectors and, in 1968, the firm set up its first professional leisure trade show in southern California. In 1971, Garrett had improved the stability of his metal detectors by eliminating the drift of the oscillator and the search coil, a first innovation which will be taken up by the competition a few years later. The Zero Drift revolution has placed Garrett at the forefront of metal detection technology for the general public.

Charles then invented the first low-cost metal detector, the famous "Mini-Hunter". It was the company's first transmitter-receiver metal detector. Garrett has also started distributing the Gravity Trap Gold Pan. In 1978, in a context where gold prices had reached a record level, Garrett received requests to open international concessions. The first store outside the United States Garrett was opened in London. In 1979, Garrett created the International Treasure Hunting Society, sponsoring treasure hunts around the world and also benefiting from great media coverage in the four corners of the planet.

In 1980, the company published its first newsletter, which continues to this day, with treasure hunt stories, technical tutorials, and humor posts. In 1984, Garrett developed a metal detector for the 1984 Olympic Games, which took place in Los Angeles. The company also provided training and security metal detectors for the National Republican Party Convention, the Pan American Games, and the 1988 Olympic Games in Seoul, South Korea.

After obtaining the first American patent for the use of microprocessors in metal detectors in 1982, Garrett presented the first microprocessor-controlled detector in 1990. That year, Garrett continued his safety training work with the armed forces Americans in Kuwait.

In 1992, Garrett provided training in security metal detectors for the Barcelona Olympics and immediately introduced the first "talking" metal detector. During the 1990s, the company also introduced the target graphical imaging metal detector (GTI) with digital signal processing (DSP). The firm then continues with a new multi-channel metal detector. The pioneering company is also called upon to ensure security at the 1996 and 2000 Olympic Games.

Over the past two decades, and in addition to ensuring the safety of major sporting events, Garrett has manufactured several new products in response to growing demand in the world of metal detection and large ground prospecting. public. In 2001, the company introduced the "Super Wand" portable metal detector. In 2003, Garrett introduced the "PD 6500i" direct-through metal detector with 33 separate point areas, including left, right, and center detection.

More recently, Garrett launched new leisure metal detectors for the "ACE" series, such as the ACE 350 in the United States and EuroACE ™ for the Old Continent. We are also witnessing the launch of the new portable security detector "Super Scanner V".

Garrett continued his successful series of launches with the redesigned "Super Scanner® V" handheld metal detector and the CSI Pro ™ ground search and security detector for law enforcement. In terms of entertainment, Garrett's most recent innovations have given birth to the Pro-Pointer which, according to the company, has become the world's best-selling metal detector.

XP Deus metal detectors

The founders of the XP Deus brand, the Frenchman Alain Loubet and his brother, bought their first metal detector when they were young. They will then become eminent treasure hunters! A classic start for a manufacturer of metal detectors, finally.

About 17 years later, XP Metal Detectors released its first hand-assembled metal detectors in a house in Loubet. The profits from the first sales are invested in hiring employees: the Loubet siblings give themselves the means to achieve their ambitions. Two years later, an XP Adventis, the brand's first metal detector, was launched in specialist stores. In this period, with its depth of detection and its ability to discriminate metals, this machine impresses.

The same year, XP (the brand name before it became XP Deus) began selling its metal detectors internationally, via its first European resellers. The XP Deus metal detector, which gave its name to the brand, was launched on the market in 2009. Light, fast, wireless, and with a good metal discrimination capacity, this detector is still considered the 'one of the recurring bestsellers on the market.

A MINELAB detector is not just any detector. The brand stands out on the careful design of its detectors, but also and above all on innovative and specific characteristics. Whether you are a detection expert or a novice, Minelab offers devices for all types of research!

Why choose a MINELAB detector?

The Australian manufacturer offers a wide range of detectors. Expert since the late 80s, Minelab has ventured where other brands had never gone. This is how we have seen devices appear with new technologies or futuristic designs (for their time).

The advantages of a Minelab detector

If you have one of these machines to detect, you are surely well informed. Indeed, the brand inspires all the confidence which is due to it. Known by many prospectors, Minelab detectors have been proven for years. Whether you are looking for a conventional VLF detector, a detector for gold, or a detector for underwater excavations and beaches, you will find everything you need at Minelab. There is a lot of feedback and the results are very good. The firm's detectors are convincing to users. Robust and reliable, they are guaranteed up to 5 years.

The innovation of Minelab detectors

The technology on some devices is staggering. In particular with FBS (Full Band Spectrum) detectors or BBS (Broad Band Spectrum) detectors. MINELAB detectors are the precursors of these innovative systems patented by Minelab in person! This process makes the detectors ultra-effective on wet beaches or highly mineralized soils!

These BBS and FBS technologies allow the detector to work on several frequencies simultaneously ranging from 1.5 kHz to 100 kHz. These systems are found in particular on the SAFARI, the E-TRAC, the EXPLORER and the EXCALIBUR II.

For the search for native gold, pulsed induction detectors develop all the power and precision necessary to help you find a gold nugget hidden underground. The look and ergonomics are also talked about. With each novelty, a Minelab detector seems to come from the future. The often clean lines and the performances are there.

How to choose the most suitable Minelab detector?

We must first ask the right questions. For some prospectors the experience must be taken into account, the places on which you plan to prospect also, of course, it will also be necessary to compose according to your budget. Here are some devices that will give you an overview to make your choice.

The best Minelab detector for beginners

To start the detection, it is not necessary to take the high-end. It makes sense to stick to detectors under 500 euros. The GO-FIND 20, 40, or 60 series is particularly appreciated. Accessible on a very small budget, they have everything you need to start detection in good conditions. The X-TERRA 305 and X-TERRA 505 are less attractive, but the quality is good. They are more efficient in the field. After a few months or a few years of practice, nothing prevents you from storing or reselling your device to invest in a better detector.

High-end Minelab detectors

Continuous with ever more performance and versatility, the X-TERRA 705 is an excellent device! He bows to the famous SAFARI. The latter is powerful, precise, and easy to use. The research is done in multi-frequencies, which makes the device stable and effective on any type of soil. Even mineralized soils or wet beaches. The ETRAC, with its 28 simultaneous frequencies is even more advanced, and better on difficult soils!

At the top of the basket, the CTX 3030 or EQUINOX. In addition to the previous ones, these metal detectors have the possibility of going completely underwater. However, I do not classify them in the category of underwater detectors because the depth remains limited to a few meters. Versatility is essential for these high-end devices. Very comfortable on the wet beach or in plowing, you can search anywhere with these!

A Minelab detector to find gold

The 3 best detectors that the brand offers to search for native gold are pulsed induction devices. These specific detectors are expensive, but they are professional equipment. The SDC 2300, the GPX 4500, GPX 5000, or GPZ 7000 will delight the seekers of gold nuggets!

The last 3 are the best known (you can often see them in some TV reports) because they came out earlier. Gold zones have no secrets for these detectors cut for the precious yellow metal.

The underwater Minelab detector

To complete the brand's collection, a Minelab detector was needed to probe the seabed. It is not cut for surface research. It is heavier than conventional devices and you would quickly be tired when sweeping on the surface. But underwater the weight of the EXCALIBUR II will be unimportant.

TESORO detector, high-performance detectors for enthusiasts!

The TESORO detector is in some ways the detector of purists! This brand is one of the oldest in the detection world. These devices take advantage of advanced technology, which has made it possible to design very powerful and super robust detectors. No artifice in the design, the goal of the American manufacturer is to offer high-performance metal detectors.

TESORO detector powerful and efficient metal detector

Why buy a TESORO detector?

When it comes to choosing a metal detector, it's important to know what you want to do with it.

With a Tesoro detector, we make sure we have good quality equipment.

The advantages of a TESORO detector

Recognized for being particularly resistant, Tesoro detectors have survived the years and are a good investment. Also, the American brand offers detectors that work on a higher frequency range than other brands. This detail is not one! Indeed, with devices operating from 10 kHz up to 18 kHz for the highest frequencies, there are two main advantages. On the one hand, the device will be better for finding small targets. Also, your Tesoro detector performs better on mineralized soils.

The other big strength of the brand is the precision of discrimination. All Tesoro detectors benefit from a high-performance screen!

Quality specific to Tesoro detectors:

The particularity of Tesoro is the absence of a large LCD screen (unlike other brands). This is also why I speak of a detector cut for detection purists. Only the sound will give you the indication to know whether to dig or not!

It should be emphasized that the fact of detecting without being disturbed by visual indications makes it possible to be much more vigilant and attentive to sound signals.

The best metal detectors from TESORO:

For his devices, this pioneer concentrates a well-honed technology in a control box reduced in size. You benefit from light and well-balanced detectors for maximum comfort during use.

Beginner TESORO detectors:

All of the brand's detectors can be used by any type of prospector. The control unit is small. Also, Tesoro is super well balanced. Therefore, each device is perfect for prolonged use. No need to have big arms to use it. Even the youngest among us can indulge in the pleasures of prospecting for leisure.

The Compadre:

It is the smallest model from TESORO. This detector already has the qualities and performance of devices in the higher range. No device on the control box, the brand goes to the essentials, good description, big power, and excellent performance for this entry-level which runs at 12 kHz!

The Silver Saber (exists in pro version):

This entry-level device is one of the most requested. Its ease of use is ideal whether you are a beginner or experienced. The Tesoro Silver Saber is clocked at 10 kHz for research. Its capabilities are excellent in terms of power but also in terms of discrimination. It is the brand's best-selling detector! It is notably the Tesoro Silver Saber which benefited the first from this miniaturization, with all the success that we know.

The Cibola

Another perfect detection device to initiate our leisure. Less known than the previous one, it nevertheless has all the qualities necessary to effectively detect! It's a very affordable price for such quality makes it a device of the first choice given its performance. Particularly precise and stable, it searches at 14KHz. This frequency is an excellent compromise between power and searches for precision. This ability to adapt to any type of terrain makes it a detector of choice.

TESORO detectors for the most experienced:

Of course, if the brand offers entry-level, it also has much more sophisticated devices.

The Tejon

A concentrate of power with extreme precision. The Tejon detector leaked a lot of ink as soon as it arrived on the market. He is comfortable on any type of terrain and his abilities on the ground are simply monstrous. Here again, you don't buy a colorful design with glitter. No! Tesoro has set the bar high in performance for this high-end detector. The price is also very competitive!

The Deleon

This is the only exception to the rule. A small screen on the control unit for reading information. Well, it's not a touch screen or 4K screen either. Emphasis is placed on the power and selectivity of the detector. The Deleon detector is one of the best detectors of the brand!

The easy Gold, the gold detector from Tesoro:

Like any good brand of detectors, Tesoro offers a model specially cut to find gold. The Easy Gold detector rotates on a search frequency of 18 kHz. Its precision coupled with its power allows it to extract the precious metal without difficulty. Very effective for all types of excavation, Easy Gold is one of the best TESORO detectors.

The Tiger Shark, the aquatic detector:

Another name announcing big power. Without a bad pun, this detector specifically made for underwater research behaves like a fish in the water. Its low weight allows it to accompany you on land, in the water, or underwater to find everything that goes under its disc. The Tiger Shark detector is perfectly capable of detecting on wet sand beaches or dry sand. Mineralization of the soil presents no problem with this high-end device. It also offers you the possibility of going up to 50 meters deep. On inland, underwater. The extent of the playground is endless for this underwater detector.

Our opinion on the TESORO detector brand:

The brand has established itself over time as one of the industry leaders. No wonder, with detectors whose weight is around 1.2 kg and technology to reduce remote control extremely. Tesoro to mix, ergonomics, and performance. Tesoro UDMs love this brand for its undeniable qualities. In general, the TESORO detector is not a toy, it is a device made for detection that will delight enthusiasts, beginners, and the most passionate and assiduous.

FISHER® RESEARCH LABS

A Fisher detector is a trustworthy device. The different models offer you the possibility of detecting any type of terrain whether you are a beginner or a detection specialist. These detectors are reputed to be powerful and robust to allow detection in excellent conditions.

Why buy a FISHER detector?

The Fisher brand is very well known in the world of metal detection. The reason is simple, it was born in 1931 in the United States. Suffice to say that Fisher detectors have had the opportunity to improve over time. Fisher was not born from the last rain and offers a wide range of detectors perfect for beginners but also devices made for more specific excavation. The Fisher detectors are guaranteed for 2 years.

Advantages of FISHER detectors:

The American brand is simply a reference among UDM (metal detector users). Its detectors are popular, they are known to be super powerful and hyper robust. Beyond a good reputation, Fisher offers a panel of detectors for each type of prospector. All devices have a large LCD screen with handling that is simple and quick. Find what to look for in the fields, in the forest, on the beach, or even in the seabed. Fisher detectors are there to find gold, scrap, bronze, or any other type of metal.

Choose a Fisher detector to start:

These devices are efficient and benefit from all the know-how of the manufacturer. Their use is easy as pie. These devices are perfect for the most common use of detectors.

The Fisher F2, F4, and F5 detectors were until recently a benchmark. In 2015 they were revised and corrected to be replaced by the Fisher F11, F22, and F44 detectors. However, these frying pans are still good devices today. They enjoy their reputation and conform to what is expected of the brand. Powerful, robust, great autonomy, and ease of use. Equipped with a display screen they are intended for beginners and people who wish to change the device or move upmarket.

The old Fisher range:

Still topical, this range deserves our full confidence. Analysis of targets is made easier thanks to the LCD screen and multi-tones. These devices have undeniable qualities and are perfect for starting detection at low costs. There is adjustable discrimination, the notch for squeezing certain targets, the conductivity index (from 0 to 99) for a pre-analysis of the target before even digging. The ground effects are adjustable for the Fisher F4 and the F5. For the Fisher F5, you can even view on the screen a soil mineralization value for optimum adjustment.

The new Fisher detectors:

The Fisher F11, Fisher F22, and Fisher F44 series arrived in 2015. This series incorporates all the strengths of the previous range (F2, F4, and F5). Of course, these new FISHER detectors have evolved. The performance has increased tenfold thanks to new technologies. The options remain much the same.

A Fisher detector from this new range offers settings that are more precise and an improved search disc. This results in better performance in detecting. The counterpart is a slightly higher price, but still very reasonable.

Fisher, high-end detectors

As I said above, the FISHER brand has detectors made for conventional detection, on poorly mineralized soils. These easy-to-use devices will suit any beginner or insider prospector. For those who already have a little shop or people who just want to have an even better Fisher detector, the American company offers 2 high-end detectors.

The FISHER F19 and FISHER F75 are VLF metal detectors with a higher frequency. The options available as well as the possible settings are much more advanced. The search frequency is 19 kHz for the F19, which makes it very efficient on small targets. It will also be better on the mineralized ground. This Fisher detector is much better for finding gold. The F75 is clocked at 13 kHz. Which allows it to be super versatile. The device retains a good power to penetrate the ground, also, it takes advantage of a frequency high enough to overcome the effects of soil and find targets that other detectors would not find. These 2 Fisher detectors are perfect for those looking for more performance and more versatility.

The Fisher GOLD BUG detector, gold detector:

The Fisher Gold Bug is the brand's gold detector. It is particularly appreciated by native gold seekers. Indeed for a price much more attractive than its competitors, this Fisher detector offers great performance. Super light, it remains easy to use and has good comfort of use. Equipped with a 27cm HDD, its power allows you to find objects in depth. The real quality of this 19 kHz detector is its ability to overcome the mineralization of the soil. On gold lands, many devices are unable to remain stable and prevent false signals. The ground effects are manually adjustable on the Gold Bug, so you can look for gold nuggets in Australia or Africa. Of course, detection on our floors is largely possible, with impressive performance too.

A Fisher detector for the beach or diving:

If you like to crisscross the beaches with your detector, you are aware that on dry sand, it is easy, on wet sand, it is another matter. To meet your needs, Fisher offers 3 specialized detectors for beach research or going underwater.

The specialist beach detector:

The CZ-3D is the preferred detector for beach detection. This multi-frequency rotates between 5 and 15 kHz. Ideal for digging on dry or wet sand, it does not encounter any difficulty on this type of hyper-mineralized soil. Very comfortable on all other terrains, its multi-tone and the multitude of settings will be quickly mastered by all users. This device is aimed at both beginners and pros. Huge potential.

Submersible Fisher detector.

The Fisher 1280-X Aquanaut is a high-performance mid-range. By definition, this detector for underwater research is submersible. You can go up to more than 75 meters to search the seabed, wrecks... etc. Monotonous, it is clocked at 2.4KHz and requires slower scanning. Underwater this sweep will naturally be slower. On the beach or more classic terrain, you just have to remember. Its small working frequency makes it possible to detect at great depths. Its submersible headset has the same capacities (75m).

The best detector for diving

The last in the series is the Fisher CZ-21. This Fisher underwater detector is a top of the range. A benchmark in the field of aquatic detection, its price is quite high. That said, performance level, you will hardly find better to prospect underwater. Waterproof with its headphones up to more than 75 meters, it works in multi-frequencies and multi-tones, just like the CZ-3D. Guaranteed penetration into the ground with this powerful Fisher detector. On the beach or other terrains, no problem for the CZ-21, this high-end detector has all the characteristics for increased performance. In the open air, only its weight does not play in its favor. It is perfect for underwater detection or beach edges.

Chapter Three

Treasure Hunting Tools and Accessories

When you are starting, it is rather advisable to opt for objects that you already have at home. But if you were to buy a single item, it will be the quality pointer.

All about the pointer

You must be wondering what a pointer is? Do not panic, we will explain everything to you. A pointer is a small, portable metal detector that allows you to locate your target precisely. So, while your metal detector will locate a target within a few centimetres, a separate pointer will indicate the exact location of the object detected.

How to use a pointer

After digging your grip, take your pointer and put it in the hole.

Once you are within a few inches of discovery, your pointer will beep (or vibrate).

Why are pointers so precious?

Simply put, they allow you to dig up your finds 10 times faster, which means you can spend more time detecting and less time digging. Also, saving time means more discoveries at the end of the day. It's that simple.

What is the best pointer?

Although there isn't much debate about it (although some people have their preferences), the best pointer is the Garrett Pro-Pointer AT. If the latter does not fit into your budget, you can perfectly opt for the little brother called Garrett Pro-Pointer II.

Another piece of equipment you will need during your research is none other than the shovel.

Shovels

In public parks, beaches, private lawns: use a small hand shovel. We recommend Lesche's digging tool.

In woods, agricultural fields, large properties without well-kept lawns: use an intermediate level shovel like the Lesche Sampson, Relic

On beaches: use a sand shovel. Don't bother with plastic unless you want it to break the first time you use it. Speaking of breakage, don't use a hand shovel unless you want to break your back.

In rocky areas: use a hand pick with a hand shovel.

In rivers: if you are looking for relics, use a hand pickaxe with a strong magnet attached to the end of the handle. This will allow you to easily pick up ferrous and magnetic targets without having to see them through the water. For non-ferrous targets in rivers, a hand shovel is often your best choice. Serious river hunters will often use a diving mask and snorkel.

It is also important to note that when you opt for a digging object, it is imperative to put a higher budget on it. So you will have a much better shovel. The cheap shovels that you can get in big box stores today break too easily.

The only brand of the shovel I can recommend is Lesche. These shovels are made in the United States. They are also first-rate and of good quality. With heat-treated steel and aeronautical grade tubes, they are the Rolls-Royce of excavators.

The next object that we will detail is simply the headphones.

All about headphones

Although headsets come with most mid to high-end detectors, they don't often come with entry-level machines. You need a headset. Everything is relative. If you are doing this for fun or just in your garden, you don't need a header. However, if you go further in your research, you will need one.

Why do you need a headset?

Contrary to what many people think of detection, the correct way to identify a target is to listen to audio signals and not to use the visual display on the LCD screen. Visual indicators serve as a complement to audio and should not be used as the primary means of identification. For this reason, you should make sure you hear what your detector is telling you. You cannot allow outside noises such as traffic, wind, or howling children to interfere with the sounds emitted by your detector. This is especially true on beaches, the sound of wind and waves can be quite loud.

Another element to take into account is quite simply the protective cover.

Protective covers

Protective covers are available for some brands of detectors like Minelab and Tesoro, but not on others like Garrett, Fisher, and Tekentics. The spool covers are used to protect the spool from scratches and stains. Excessive wear and tear on one coil can significantly affect its performance, and you will be forced to purchase another coil. Generally speaking, a protective cover costs no more than $15. It is not expensive to pay to protect your items.

Pouches / transport bags / backpacks

The pockets that connect to your belt are essential in my opinion. If you plan on leaving for a metal detection session of only 20 minutes, then yes, you can probably put everything in your pockets. Anything beyond that you are going to want a wallet.

Do not forget the things that you will take with you: finds, trash cans, shovel, pointer, toothbrush, car keys, and everything else you want to put in them. We also find that carrying-bags are important equipment. The main difference between a carrying-bag and a backpack is that with most of these, you will need to break your detector to hold it. This means disconnecting and unraveling the wire from the coil, then decomposing your detector into 3 pieces, for my taste it is a waste of time.

The transport bags are much longer and allow you to install your entire detector without having to dismantle it. A huge time saver and much less headache. The only times I would recommend using a backpack are if you are hiking or biking long distances to reach your detection destination.

In summary: all the equipment you need

- First aid kit
- Spare batteries (for detector and pointer)
- Solar cream
- Insect repellent
- Gloves
- Parts field guide
- Battery charger (if using rechargeable batteries)
- Pocket knife / multi-tool
- Whistle (in case you meet a wild animal)
- A case for precious finds

Choosing a Metal Detector

This device accompanies you in your gold rush, helping you to detect metallic objects of value (or not). More than just a machine, the metal detector is potentially a tool for enrichment, as long as you have the motivation, the skill, and above all the luck it takes!

The criteria for choosing the right metal shredder can give you a hard time because we are staying in a rather technical field. This section offers a complete file to help you choose the right metal detector.

How to Choose a Metal Detector

To properly choose your metal detector, you will have to follow a checklist of the selection criteria which is mainly technical. But before that, it will be necessary to define the type of objects which you wish to seek, because certain models have "specialties". Parts and relics in the ground, detection of metals underwater or in wet environments, and the prospect of precious metals (gold).

You must then look at the criterion of discrimination. This is the ability of your metal detector to distinguish between the desired target and an unwanted target such as metal waste (soda cans, nails, etc.). The more a metal detector can discriminate between types of metals, the less you will have to dig unnecessarily.

The third criterion to take into account is the ground balance. You should know that all soils contain a small (natural) concentration of metal, especially iron. The best metal detectors can ignore this metal concentration so as not to emit unwanted signals. Ideally, opt for a metal detector capable of assigning a different tone to each type of metal. This will allow you to improve your soil prospecting experience.

You should also take into account the technology embedded in your metal detector. Most of the mainstream and inexpensive models operate on the principle of low frequencies. If your practice is more serious, we strongly advise you to opt for a pulse induction metal detector. To go further, you can consult our metal detector buying guide.

Should you buy a new or used metal detector?

This is a legitimate question since a good metal detector can cost several thousand dollars. But here it is: as with all machines, the second-hand market presents both opportunities and scams. To make the right choice, we will have to review several criteria that we have compiled in this dedicated section.

Like professionals, the most passionate amateurs regularly change models, which allows a certain dynamism on the second-hand market. You will be able to make great savings, provided you follow our selection list to the letter. The search coil, the electronic part, and the handle of the detector constitute the golden triptych to acquire a well-used metal detector. To carry out your transaction, we advise you to meet the seller in a public and lively place, for obvious security reasons.

You also have the option of online sales platforms like Amazon. Certainly, you're not going to be able to test the device (although you can always request very detailed videos from serious sellers). But you will be able to consult the opinions posted by the users and make your own opinion on the seriousness of your interlocutor.

How much does a metal detector cost?

Any leisure has a cost... but in the case of the metal detector, the situation is a little special. Admittedly, the initial investment can be substantial if you choose a good model with pulsed induction, endowed with a beautiful sensitivity, and an excellent capacity of discrimination. However, metal detection and soil prospecting are activities that can potentially bring you money, which will allow you to make your purchase more or less quickly, depending on your attendance and persistence.

Several factors impact the price of metal detectors: the brand, the duration of the manufacturer's warranty, the typology of targets detected by the device, R&D costs as well as the technology embedded in the machine. An intermediate quality metal detector for amateurs will cost on average between 700 and 2,000 dollars, while a professional quality metal detector will cost more than 4,000 dollars.

What about professional metal detectors?

In addition to its use for recreational purposes, the metal detector remains an everyday device for many professionals. It is particular to professionals working in particular in security (airports, buildings, events), in the recovery of lost objects, in archaeological exploration, in geological research, or mine clearance operations. As in all segments that involve an electronic part, the metal detector market has seen the border between amateur and professional devices gradually fade. Nevertheless, professional detectors, or at least serious, share certain characteristics: the possibility of manual parameter setting of all the detection variables, automatic presets to go faster, a backlit LCD screen, touch controls, wireless headphones to clearly distinguish tones, digital radio connectivity, a potentiometer to adapt to soil mineralization, etc.

What is the best metal detector?

The entry-level selection aside, let's talk about the best metal detector. There isn't a better metal detector. It all depends on what you need. Some people will tell you that some metal detectors are easier to use and they find more relics. Yes, but the difference is mainly played on the price at which you will buy your metal detector. It is not possible to compare a detector at $100 and another at $2500, for example.

Nevertheless, it is better to ask yourself: which metal detector would suit me best? To be able to answer this question, different elements must be taken into account:

- Your place of residence.
- The region in which you plan to search for metals.
- The type of detection you want to practice.
- Your budget.
- Your level of experience.
- Are you tech-savvy?

But as you can imagine, all the metal detectors do the same thing: it detects metal. What makes some detectors more expensive than others is the additional functionality and the different technologies they provide. Let's take an example: if a coin is in front of you, whether you have a $100 or $2,500 metal detector, the result will be the same. But if we put an old rusty nail next to the room. The $100 detector will detect metal, but will not be able to differentiate between the workpiece and the nail. A good detector at $2500 will go so far as to tell you that there are two different metal objects in front of you, one which is a coin and one which is junk. So that's all you need to know to select an entry-level detector. You can't go wrong with the ones I mentioned above, so make your choice and go for it. A final point to note is that there is a huge market for used metal detectors. So if your budget is a little tight but you don't want to settle for a poorer quality detector, consider buying a used one.

Understanding important indicators of underground metal detectors

As an underground detection device, underground detectors are very strange for most people. They play an extremely important role in many areas

such as underground exploration, pipeline detection, and protection against military explosions.
Their quality is measured by a very large number of
indicators. Therefore, I will briefly introduce some
of the important indicators below.

The main indicators are the depth of detection, the
adjustment of the ground balance, the detection
mode, the size of the detection disc, and the
endurance. One of the most important indicators of
underground metal detectors is the depth of
drilling. Many unscrupulous businessmen, to better
sell the company's products, the product
performance deliberately exaggerated, say can
detect ten meters, tens of meters, it is impossible. In
this regard, consumers must be sure to keep their
eyes open, not to be blinded by the so-called virtual
depth. The current state of knowledge, the best
underground metal detector in the world, can detect
3 meters, it is already very good.

In addition to an underground metal detector deep
sounding, there is one most important parameter:
balance adjustment. Adjusting the soil balance, that
is to say by adjusting the reference value inside the
detector, is better suited to different soils. Can
effectively eliminate signal interference caused by

mineralization reaction, improve detection efficiency.

Different detection modes can also lead to different prices. Some detectors have nine detection modes: dynamic full metal mode, static full metal mode, default dE program, improved PF mode, CL cache positioning mode, etc. Different detection modes can be selected based on different usage scenarios and requirements, and user needs can be more precisely met

Some people think, "The larger the probe, the better." Is that the case? The answer of course is no. Smaller probes are easier to detect than larger probes and are more sensitive than large probes. In the region (such as nooks and crannies) large search coil is not easily accessible, weak discs can play small and flexible sounding, a unique advantage.

However, the extent of mineralization in the soil is weaker. The waste little open land, large research coils explored more deeply, and wider coverage can significantly increase efficiency too, with less time, completed the survey of a region.

Endurance is also an important indicator for testing the quality of an underground metal detector. Good underground metal detectors have a long service life. Archaeological members do not return home three or four days during archaeological operations and it takes a long time to inspect the site. If the endurance capacity is not good, it will be troublesome and affect the progress of the work. Therefore, from a professional point of view, long-lived underground metal detectors will be more popular with professionals.

Chapter Four

Where Should You Look For Treasure?
The best corners for detection

The most common places to use your metal detector are:

• Public parks

• Beaches

• Woods

• Garden

• Rivers

• Fields

However, you must take care to always be authorized to detect metals where you wish to do so. The use of detectors in places without permission is prohibited by law. Each plot of land belongs to someone and each time authorization is imperative!

For example, many public parks strictly prohibit metal detection - especially the parks run by the county and the state. And you can assume that federal parks are also prohibited. So always check with the town hall before leaving to prospect. When prospecting in the woods or fields, be sure to watch the property lines. It is not difficult to get lost and spill over onto someone else's private property.

Finally, let's talk about private property. Hunting on private property will be by far the best terrain for several reasons:

No one has ever been there.

The owner can give you clues to detect many metals. Maybe they noticed broken pottery in the woods years ago. It would be a great place to start detection.

In any case, you must obtain permission for this type of land. Also, it is preferable to opt for a written authorization, rather than a verbal one, although the latter is sufficient. Take written permission (be it a letter or a printed email) and keep it with you at all times during your hunt. In this way, if you are approached by someone, you have proof that you are authorized to be there.

What is the best corner to detect?

Metal detectors bring out our adventurer and explorer side. If certain detection spots require the use of a specific detector, most of the land to be surveyed is done with most devices. I will tell you about some specifics later. If the image that we have most often in mind when we talk about metal detectors is that of the beach, it is quite possible to find interesting finds in the forest, in a park, in the middle vineyards or the fields.

Forest detection

The forest is one of the most coveted places for detection. There are several reasons for this. You can find everything there, often in good condition and you are sheltered from views and days with capricious weather. Also, the forest is full of characteristic points to make our work easier. I will talk about this later. If you are considering using a detector in the woods, there are a few things to know.

The advantages of forest detection

On the one hand, tranquillity will be required. There is little or no car, noise, or walkers. This allows you to have a maximum calm to fully enjoy your outing. Also, snow, rain, and wind or a blazing sun are much less demanding and restrictive when prospecting under tree cover.

On the other hand, it must be remembered that forests have not always been forests. Before the excessive use of fertilizers, your forest may have been a cultivated field. As a result, coins and other objects that were lost or intentionally hidden tens of years or even centuries ago have probably kept a beautiful appearance and will display beautiful patinas when you take them out of the ground. Without fertilizer or machine tools for plowing, you are more likely to find objects well preserved in the forest, without traces of excessive oxidation or unfortunate shocks.

The disadvantages of the forest

Ticks are often the worst enemy when detected in the forest. I'm not talking about cobwebs or mosquitoes, but it can also be problematic quickly. The other annoying point is the proximity of the trees in certain woods which prevents us from sweeping over a large area fluidly. To this must be added the roots of the trees which can be particularly troublesome and prevent us from digging easily.

The beach is a special playground, so you have to know which detector to use for the beach. It is divided into two distinct zones. The dry sand beach, accessible and passable for all metal detectors. The wet sand beach, which requires more specific equipment or good quality detectors with the possibility of adequate settings for this type of soil, is difficult to prospect!

The benefits of beach detection

The first positive point of detection on the beach is that it is easy. The ground is flat, there are no branches, no big furrows of the earth which makes you lose an enormous depth of research. Everything is done so that you find what is underground. The beach is the ideal place to find coins or to find jewelry. If you decide to prospect on a large beach frequented by full tourists, it is a safe bet that they will have dropped a small piece when buying ice cream or a donut. Suffice to say that this room will not be lost for everyone if you go through there.

On the one hand, people often remove their jewelry (necklaces, bracelets, and rings) to go in the water or to pass the sunscreen and thus avoid bad tan marks. If they keep them on, nature sometimes helps them remove them. This is particularly true with rings. Indeed, water is cooler than air in general. So by going into the water to cool off, the muscles and the skin relax. As a result, finger size decreases significantly. In the end, the rings slide easily with your finger to get lost under a thin layer of sand.

Finally, the beach is a gold mine in the sense that every year, or every month or even every week or every day for the busiest beaches, you are likely to find a crowd of valuables. Particularly pieces and jewelry, and hopefully telephones or watches. Remember that civility does not kill. And these objects can be deposited at the town hall which will return them in the event of a declaration of loss. If after a certain time, nobody comes to claim them, then they will belong to you.

The disadvantages of the beach

The beaches are full of finds. However, it is not uncommon to come across capsules or aluminum foil or cans. This multitude of waste can quickly become painful.

Certain beaches are prohibited for detection by municipal decree. This is often linked to the crowds of these beaches which welcome several thousand people every day. Very often, these municipal decrees allow prospecting on the beach at preferential time slots. This is in order not to disturb the vacationers. Reasonably, you can hope to detect early in the morning or at the end of the day. You need to be well informed before putting yourself outside the law.

This is irrespective of landing beaches which are, of course, prohibited from prospecting. It is prohibited by law. On the one hand, these beaches are closely linked to history. On the other hand, there are potential remains of unexploded ordnance or barbed wire or other decaying ferrous on these old battlefields. The danger is omnipresent.

Lastly, since there are many tourists or walkers, a beach trip can quickly become a question and answer game for long minutes. Nothing bad in itself, people are interested or just curious. They may even ask you to drop by.

Advice for detecting on the beach

If your detector allows, the wetland area is more conducive to interesting finds. To identify the right part of the beach to detect, look on the sand. You will probably find a kind of line that slightly marks the border between dry and wet beaches. Very often, you will even see deposits or waste discharged by the sea. It can be small pieces of wood, algae, or even black sand. This indication gives you the limit of rising waters.

Secondly, the best time to practice your leisure is very early in the morning or the evening. Why? First of all, you will not disturb anyone. Tourists like to have their peace of mind, that's why they take vacations. So if you circulate between the towels you will inevitably frustrate some. Therefore, it's easier for you when no one is there. The slalom between holidaymakers is not made to optimize the area to be detected in a given time. Finally, there is the screener. This machine, often pulled by a tractor, smooths the beach to make it look like new. Beyond giving a beautiful appearance to the beach, the screen picker collects the waste lost the previous days. The ideal, you understand it is to pass before the latter. In general, it passes at sunrise, but it is not everywhere the same.

Detection in the fields

It is one of the essential facets of detection. Easy and pleasant to prospect, if you start from the principle that all fields reserve their small batch of surprises. To tell the truth, I find it difficult to leave a field until I have released a coin, a button, or a loop. All the detectors are good for prospecting in the fields. You should always ensure to ask for authorization before going into a field to make some small holes. It is rare for owners to take a dim view of the fact that you come to pick up a few coins, not to mention that you will be removing pounds of waste to get there. Also, if you do not have an experienced eye, you may detect in a field that has already been inspected. Beyond the lack of civility, it will not surprise you to have trouble with the owner. Let's see the things to remember before you get started.

The advantages of fields

Generally returned every year, if a field gives a good year (a lot of finds), there is a good chance that you will do many more the following year. By turning the earth upside down, plows and other agricultural machinery allow objects to resume breathing on the surface (within the first 20 centimeters). Thus, your detector will be able to find these recently reappeared objects. The advantage is that even detectors for beginners or entry-level will be enough to get out a lot of finds.

Fields are a bit like the perfect playground. In fact, in the right season, the earth has been turned upside down or even crumbled finely in the best of cases. Therefore, passing with the detector by sweeping from left to right is done without difficulty. No roots, tree trunks, or large stones to avoid. Also, to make our work easier, we often see traces of tractor wheels or the furrows of plowing tools on the ground. This allows them to be followed (as in a corridor) without risking passing and passing several times on the same line.

Little tip by the way, if a field is too large, you can put a marker at the end of the last detected line (a stick planted or a small pile of stones will do the trick). Like this, coming back a few days later, you will quickly know where to start prospecting again. You can also leave your shovel lying on the ground. It will leave a fine mark on the ground, and you will be able to see where you have already gone. For that of course, it will be necessary that the ground lends itself to it.

The disadvantages in the fields

The biggest constraint is that in a field, unlike a forest or a beach, the detection window is done quickly. Indeed, if we take the example of corn or wheat fields, at best, we can detect 6 months in the year. If the field is set aside after harvest until the next time it is sown, it leaves you only in late summer, fall, and winter to explore. That said, it's already not bad. Some fields are quickly grown after harvest. This allows farmers to optimize the yields of their land.

I draw your attention to the interest of requesting authorization from the owner. Especially if the field is freshly sown because, in addition to not respecting the law, you risk damaging the future crops of the farmer. It is not the objective of detection, nor the ethics of the prospector.

If we are talking about seeds, you are aware that the majority of farmers use fertilizers and/or pesticides. It's a shame for the finds because the most fragile will not resist long contact with certain chemicals. Any treasure which has spent several hundred years on the ground without being damaged too much may perhaps have the appearance of a bar of soap thanks to these products. Finding a piece is great, but when it's damaged the pleasure loses a little of its flavor.

Finally, prospecting in the fields is good because they are often clear, flat, and easy to dig. The downside is that you are also very visible from afar. It is not a big concern because you will detect with the authorization of the owner, I do not doubt it. However, you will attract the curious who will come to see you to ask you what you are doing or to find out if you have found a treasure. Nothing too bad, when we say that certain meetings allow us to know certain points of details of the prospective place. The elders will remember the land, and it is not uncommon to be told where to pass the old path that led to the village, or that there were a mill 2 steps from here ... etc. It's just that after 2 hours of detection, you quickly spent 1-hour chatting... and therefore finding nothing during this time. Take the bright side, you may have gleaned valuable information from such an area.

The vines are a great place to detect. The soil is often turned over there to aerate the soil and thus optimize the crops. Very often, we come across great finds there. Especially if the farm you are going to has been a vineyard for a long time. It has not been that long since humans have been using machines to harvest grapes. So for centuries, it was done by hand. This is why it is not uncommon to find very old coins in the rows of vines. You will find pebbles in the ground, but the digging operation is not done as easily.

The advantage of vines

The big highlight of the vines in comparison with a more traditional field is that it is accessible all year round. In summer or winter, no worries, the rows of vines are a real land of welcome for prospectors, subject to being authorized.

The rows of vines greatly facilitate the work for your research. Just follow a row and move onto the next row when you're at the end of the line. So you will not spend fifty times in the same place. Each year and sometimes several times a year, the soil is turned deep, bringing up a lot of objects on the surface, and that's all beneficial for the prospector who goes there.

Just like in the fields, care must be taken to have the owner 's authorization to prospect in the vineyards. By explaining that you do not touch the vine plants in any way, or by promising to remove some waste from his land and fill in the small holes made, you should not be refused authorization.

The disadvantages of vines

If you are in the south and you want to detect the vines in the early morning, before it is too hot, you will probably have some cicadas that will fly over you. It surprises the first few times, but no risk, it will not eat you.

The main problem when detecting in vines is the iron stakes and the wire that connects each of the stakes. If your detector goes too close to these ferrous, you will have many false sounds. You just have to take the hit and sweep without getting too close. Anyway, the stakes will always give you the same conductivity index, and it will surely be a good big clear sound.

The last problematic point to address is not trivial. Who says vine, says grape. Prospecting in the vines in the middle of the grape season is not a good idea. If you like grapes and start eating a few grains, you may start again and again. So your detection outing in the vines can quickly turn into the grape tasting. You must resist the temptation, otherwise, you will not find anything.

Detect in the meadows

It's a bit like in the fields. Detection in the meadows is simple and pleasant. The little difference is that they sometimes serve as pasture, and the land is rarely turned over there. Often, the owners let the grass grow (up to 60 or 80 cm) and then cut it and make haystacks or bales which will be used mainly to feed the animals.

From one year to the next there has not been much change, and few new things to find, unlike a busy beach. I'm not saying you won't find anything anymore. It's just that I doubt that hundreds of coins will come to the surface in one year. If the meadows are used as pasture, care must be taken not to open the enclosures at the risk of seeing animals flee. But you will probably have the owner's instructions when asking for permission to detect in a meadow. Sometimes surrounded by electrified wire, the edges of the pastures will often be the subject of parasitic noises linked to these wires. There are two solutions to fix it. You must either move away from the wire or lower the sensitivity of the detector at the risk of losing research depth.

Detection along the paths

There is a lot to say on the roads. I'll go to the basics. It is necessary to differentiate the old paths from the recent paths. It is difficult if not impossible. However, you have to have a little flair. Access from one village to another or from one city to another a few centuries ago did not necessarily take the roads you know today. The shortest path between 2 points is the straight line, you will sometimes find paths in the forest for example which have a steep slope. This can be a good indicator of age. If it is surrounded by large trees too, it is probably because the passage has been around for a long time.

What the path offers is the advantage of having been trodden for a long time. So there are probably finds from many eras to be made. And if a path was taken by carriages of horses and pedestrians, be sure that pedestrians deviate from the path when they hear or see a horde of horses arriving. This sometimes occurs as a precaution and safety to avoid being knocked over or stepped on. But sometimes it was also out of fear of being looted or robbed. Thus, these people could quickly decide to deviate from a path and to hide their treasure in a hole or under a stone. They could even sometimes never find what they had hidden. This is where you come in! Detecting on a path is good, but remember that prospecting on the edges of the path can be even better.

Prospect in the parks

There are many things to find in the parks. It's a bit like the beach. Recent currencies often fill the bottom of our pockets after a detection trip to a park. The counterpart is that waste abounds. Between aluminum foil and a Can puller or other capsule, you will quickly be convinced that there is a passage in the park being explored. Especially the passage of the man of the 20th and 21st centuries. Even if it can be frustrating to pick up litter, you will not fail to unearth a few pieces or a small piece of jewelry lost and accidentally found by you.

Search in rivers

The rivers are regularly the object of beautiful finds. It goes from the coin thrown as an offering to the cell phone lost by falling from the canoe-kayak to the old rifle hurriedly thrown by a soldier before being taken prisoner. However, keep in mind that not all detectors go into the water. Two solutions are available to you. Either you have a detector that supports being partially or fully put underwater. Note that many devices from the entry-level can search with the disc and the bottom of the cane submerged. The other solution is to bring a magnet. Magnet fishing is becoming more and more widespread.

Other good spots that not everyone thinks of

To conclude on the corners to detect, let me present to you some spots that we do not always think of. These spots are however very conducive to make beautiful finds and some coins to satisfy your outing and not to return empty-handed.

There are transit areas for Travelers. There are many recent coins and sometimes some jewelry. On picnic areas, this is a bit like parks. To hit the bull's eye, nothing could be simpler, you just have to approach the leafiest trees. Most of the time, by prospecting in the shade of a tree around noon or 4 p.m., you are almost sure to be in the best place to find small objects fallen from the pockets of whoever came to relax and do a snack break. If the picnic area has benches with adjoining tables, it is directly above the bench that you will find the most. However, be aware that there will be more capsules than coins unless you are lucky.

Around sports fields, it's atypical but not stupid. Tell yourself that it is not uncommon to find a snack bar around a soccer field, a rugby stadium, or an equestrian center. And then like everywhere, a coin, a ring or a bracelet can fall so quickly when we heckle or play ball. For these spots, of course, I do not encourage you to go digging directly on the ground, because even if you have got into the good habit of filling your holes, it would not be correct and potentially dangerous.

Chapter Five

Where to make beautiful finds? The characteristic points

If I knew the answer, it would be luxury. But, some places are more conducive to find interesting things. In the forest, the old paths guarantee you a regular passage of travelers, who sometimes crossed the forests in a hurry. The brigands who robbed their victims often took up residence in the very heart of the forests, like the famous cave of the brigands of the Fontainebleau forest. To avoid these looters, it was not uncommon for people to take the roadsides. This avoided facing a horde of people on horseback. On the other hand, one can quite imagine that by moving on the lower sides, less passable, it was more common to lose a small room or a button of cape here and there.

The large tree trunks betray an advanced age of the tree at the foot of which some travelers have been able to doze off and lose a few objects, even hide a treasure. There are many characteristic points for burying a small purse to avoid being robbed by robbers.

The oddly shaped trees and large stones suggest an easily memorable landmark for those who want to bury a treasure in a hurry. It is a good idea to go around these areas, especially when the forests and woods are near the main axes of passage or exodus.

The bridges were obligatory crossing points to cross from one bank to another. Even a hundred years ago, many travelers saw it as an opportunity to make an offering to fulfil their wishes or simply to bring them luck during their journey.

Similarly, the crossroads are typical. They allowed certain travelers to rely on their beliefs or to influence their destiny by making an offering. A small room allowed (according to them) to guide them on the safest path. Thus they probably thought to avoid attracting the eye of the occult forces or that of the wandering vagrants and other looters.

The crossings, the trees, the particular curves of a watercourse, or the rocks ... so many particular points that allow you to find your property several days later or even years later. And sometimes, these objects are never recovered. Or by forgetting on the part of the owner, or then because the latter was no longer able to do so.

The laundries or water sources were and still are meeting places. These places were suitable for washing clothes for example. Who has never left a piece in his pants pocket by putting it in the washing machine? While the laundry was drying, you had to take care. Sewing was a key activity for useful patience. Beyond that, these are sources of water that bear witness to many prayers and wishes and therefore leading to many offerings.

The cavities are natural refuges. In case of heavy rain or storm, or to escape the sight of danger. A small cave could often be an opportunity to make a short stopover and it is, therefore, possible to lose a small object so that we prospectors would find it for ages later.

The high points could be durable implantation areas. In hostile times, the further you see, the less you can be surprised. Conversely, the low points along the thalweg lines are favorable to the proximity of watercourses. In a prosperous region, it is often where the dwellings are located.

Which detector to choose according to the terrain?

Whether on the beach, in the forest, or urban areas, the first thing to know is that there are a host of detector models. Some are small and light, others bulkier. I assure you right away, it's cheaper to choose a metal detector model for the forest than for the beach. The latter requires very specific equipment. In the forest, models that search on low frequencies are perfect. Conversely, on polluted or highly mineralized soils, high frequencies are preferred. Low or high frequency is not the only important point. Do you want to do deep or surface mass prospecting? Small or large objects? So many questions that are essential to choosing a good detector.

In general, I recommend choosing a versatile detector. Thus, the majority of grounds are available to you to detect without limit.

Code of conduct for metal detection

Here are the few rules you should follow when hunting for treasure:

1. I will respect private and public property, all historic and archaeological sites and will not detect metals on these lands without proper authorization.

2. I will keep myself informed and obey all local and national laws relating to the discovery and communication of treasures found.
3. I will assist law enforcement officials whenever possible.
4. I will not cause intentional damage to property of any kind, including fences, signs, and buildings.
5. I will always fill the holes I dig.
6. I will not destroy property, buildings, or the remains of deserted structures.
7. I will not leave garbage or other unwanted items.
8. I take with me all the trash and targets dug with me when I leave after each search area.

Landlords and government officials will no longer grant permission if you leave empty holes behind and act irresponsibly. The thing to remember is that, wherever you go to detect, you must leave this place exactly as it was before your arrival or better

Obtaining Permission on private property

For some reason, this appears to be one of the most common barriers to accessing many detection locations. Many people get nervous or stupid when they knock on someone's door asking for permission. And it is understandable in some cases.

Let's face it, metal detection is not very common in certain regions of the country, and people living in these regions may not have a clue what you are talking about.

Likewise, in more suburban areas full of beautiful, well-kept green lawns, many people might tell you to leave. After all, they have spent so much time and money on their lawns and don't want you to come and dig it up. While this can be a problem for many homes, it can sometimes help show the owner how detection works. Because if you remember our code of ethics for metal detection, you will leave the property exactly as you found it. If you don't feel comfortable knocking on someone's door to get started, some alternatives are to send them a letter, drop a flyer/business card in their mailbox, or even call by phone. Either way, just be honest and direct with them.

The most common agreement between the detector and the owner is that the prospector keeps everything he finds unless the owner specifically asks to keep something. The prospector is also required to return to the owner all lost objects, jewelry, and family objects.

Do Your Research

While the most important part of this activity is having fun, it never hurts to create more productive hunts for yourself and walk away with better finds. So instead of finding nails in your two-hour hunt, you could potentially walk away with coins and relics that are hundreds of years older.

Here are some ways to do good research:

Old maps

Search Map: Arguably the best search method, looking at old maps of your city or town can give you tons of ideas on where to look. Depending on where you live, an online tool available to the public is great for comparing old maps with current maps. You can enter any address and quickly display overlays of old maps. So, for example, I can see a current map of my house and overlay a 1950 or 1820 map to compare how the area has changed over time. This allows you to quickly identify things that no longer exist. If there was once an old house in the woods near your house or point of interest, it would be a good idea to detect it there.

It is an extremely effective way to recover lost and forgotten properties and structures. You can use it several times and get astounding results each time. The only limitation is that they do not have older data, generally, they only go back about 100 years or even 200 years at most. But if a house built in the 1700s was still standing in 1930, you should be able to spot it.

You can also easily find much older maps of your city or areas of interest from online map collections, your local library, and local historical associations. As I mentioned above, your local library will often have invaluable resources to consult. Often this material will be in a special locked room. But just ask your librarian and he'll be happy to grant you access. The same goes for local historical associations. These can often be even more effective sources of information because the people who work there can be a great asset to you. And who knows, you could even make new friends and become a member of the association.

Old maps show the configuration of a town, a region, a department over several decades or even several centuries. Among the most famous, let us quote the Map of Cassini (1683 to 1744) at the scale of 1 / 86400th (1 cm = 864 m), then the staff map (1818 to 1881) at 1 / 80000e (1 cm = 800 m).

The most recent maps are those of the National Geographic Institute (IGN). They exist on many scales, but the best informed is the map at 1 / 25000th (1 cm = 250 m). This map is a real mine of information concerning topography (relief), hydrography (watercourse), toponymy (place-names), land use (vines, orchards, woods ...). Regularly updated, these maps allow a very good location in the field.

Treasure guides specific to the region

Area Treasure Guide: Another way to find great places to spot in your area is to buy a historical book for your state or region. You can find them in your bookstore or online. But essentially, these books include things like historic sites and events, local folklore, old maps, known military battle sites/campgrounds/walking routes, and more. While these books may contain a ton of useful information, most of the information is not practical, as many sites will be banned and will require special permission or a permit. But they are certainly fun to read and better understand your region!

The owners

An often overlooked research strategy is to talk to older members of your community as well as owners of older houses/properties. Many people who like to hunt relics from the time of the Revolution often ignore this suggestion. Why? Simply because they believe that a person born in 1932 cannot know such distant information. Sometimes stories can give us great clues to discover an ancient property that we would never have found otherwise.

As I mentioned above, it often happens that owners and farmers (especially those with several hectares) remember things that could guide the location of your detection. Like the example, I gave with an owner digging up old broken pottery on a section of his land. I have seen that some owners have a brief history of the house and the land that has been passed from one owner to another. This can provide valuable clues and help you choose your detection area. Although there are many other types of research that you can do, these are often the most effective and easiest to conduct.

Archives

Since 1970, the archives of municipalities with less than 2,000 inhabitants have been kept in the Departmental Archives. The latter provide very old information and in very diverse fields (the origin of the town, organization and administrative life, religious life, economy, and society ... There are also cadastral maps, maps, and old plans, engravings, and photographs.

Museums

In addition to their educational role and thematic visits, museums have libraries on very specific subjects (Gallo-Roman, medieval, revolutionary times, etc.).

Local history

What region, what village has not had its hour of glory over the centuries thanks to an illustrious figure, a historic event, a site, a monument to the past steeped in history? There is always a scholar, a parish priest, a teacher, an association to transcribe the facts, and keep the memory of them. Where to look? In the Archives, in Town Hall, in specialized bookshops, in heritage protection associations, book fairs, flea markets.

Aerial photographs are mainly used for the design or updating of maps or plans. They reveal quantities of elements of all kinds, often invisible from the ground and not mapped. They allow you to observe not only the current state of the area photographed, but sometimes also its history! Because soils keep in memory for years, even sometimes centuries, the transformations they have undergone and which do not escape the photographic objective.

Get closer to a detection club

An important point, maybe there is a detection club in your area. It may be interesting to get closer to it. Indeed, clubs are associations of enthusiasts, and what better to learn? The advantage is that outings are regularly organized trainings and you can discuss your different finds.

Many detectorists stay in their corner without necessarily exchanging with others, except on the internet but if you have the possibility, try to give it a try in a club. You will see that it is very enriching and formative.

Chapter Six

The hunt for Gold

Most prospectors have already wondered how and where to go. Several techniques exist to find gold. The best known are gold panning, detection, and mining. I could also talk about treasure hunting, the pendulum method, or even go to a jewelry store to find the precious yellow metal so coveted. But these latter methods are not the ones we will discuss in this section. Finding gold with detectors depends initially on the nature of the gold objects you are looking for. As a general rule, gold diggers are not looking for gold teeth, even if some people are lucky to find them! No, in the search for gold, the gold miner will find a gold nugget or glitter, while the detector will find gold coins or jewelry.

Finding gold with a metal detector

As I said, the prospector can find gold in the form of coins or jewelry in most cases. Sometimes also in the form of nuggets or gold flakes depending on the type of excavation and the type of device used. You have no doubt already heard of prospectors in the gold-bearing countries such as Australia, Zimbabwe, the eastern United States with the famous gold rush, or in Niger or Canada to name only the best known. These places are full of gold in their natural state in the first centimeters of earth. Researchers specializing in this type of excavation survey large areas with their detector and often find large gold nuggets weighing several grams. For some, it is even their livelihood. This type of research requires a metal detector for gold which is often expensive but sometimes quickly pays for itself. Indeed, gold soils are often very mineralized and few devices can research these conditions.

The best detectors to find gold via pulsed induction

On these soils rich in gold, here is our selection of pulsed induction (PI) detectors. These are the most used for the detection of native gold because they are the most efficient, but they are also more expensive than VLF devices.

- ATRE by GARRETT

- GPX 5000 by Minelab or GPX 5000 by Minelab

- GOLDEN KING by NOKTA Basic version or GOLDEN KING by NOKTA Pro version

These detection devices are very efficient on gold and detect at great depths. They are freed from the mineralization of soils which are the bane of other types of detectors. For conventional detection on all types of objects, they are often less appreciated because their ability to discriminate is less.

Find gold in everyday detection

If you do not have the time or the desire to go so far to search for gold, you can always visit Europe (France Belgium, Switzerland, Germany ... etc). Leisure detection allows many prospectors to exhume a gold currency from time to time. With, each time, the intense sensation that accompanies the discovery. I say gold coin, but a gold ring is not excluded and brings as much pleasure. After all, gold has for thousands of years been the most prestigious and coveted metal in the eyes of almost everyone.

To maintain a certain versatility and sufficient performance for daily detection, a detector which holds the road is necessary. Most frying pans (VLF detectors) can find many objects. However, when it comes to getting out of gold, the high-end is to be preferred. Of course, a 20 franc gold Napoleon type coin will be found by entry-level devices. Provided it is not too deep and there is not a rusty nail or worse. A horseshoe nearby would make gold coins invisible to your detector if you discriminate against ferrous metals.

But beyond a high reactivity associated with fine discrimination, ideally, you need a high-frequency detector to optimize your chances of finding gold (14 kHz seems to be a minimum). Take the example of a small gold earring or a gold quinary (it's a very small Roman coin). This kind of rare find may have already passed 4 or 5 cm under your feet without your detector emitting any sound. A high-end detector would surely not have missed the opportunity to make you dig!

Selection of the best VLF gold detectors

These detectors have proven themselves when it comes to finding gold. These metal vacuum cleaners are formidable for probing the soil and finding buried gold!

- DEUS from XP

- AT Gold from Garrett

- XTERRA 705 from MINELAB

With this type of VLF detector, the larger your disk the less your device will be disturbed by the mineralization of the soil. However, a small disc makes gain in precision on the small targets (gold flakes or small gold nugget).

Tips for Finding Gold with a Metal Detector

Detect in all metals mode

It should not be forgotten that gold is often found in contact with other minerals and that African or Australian soils are very often less polluted than in the US. So we advise you to detect all metals, not to reject the iron, and to put the detector in "all metals" mode. This also allows you to gain depth.

Forget entry-level detectors

The search for native gold presupposes the detection of nuggets and therefore of small objects. An entry-level single-frequency VLF detector will therefore generally not do the trick. The search for small nuggets is therefore carried out up to 50cm maximum. If your nugget is bigger you can go deeper. In most cases, start with a "small" VLF type detector but with a minimum frequency of 14kHz (not below!) or a multifrequency device. Later, if you want to obtain better results or even reach certain profitability, opt for a Pulsed Induction detector. You will understand, we are not talking about "gold detector" but detectors optimized for the search for gold nuggets.

Use a large disc to cover more area

To cover more area and gain depth, you can add a large disc to your detector. These discs with diameters greater than 38cm are generally optional and designed not by the manufacturers themselves but by brands that do just that. A large disc costs between 180 and 350 dollars and is a real plus. You can acquire it at the time of purchase in a pack or much later.

Better manage your compensation for ground effects

In Africa, Australia, or the DOM-TOM (volcanic lands), the soils are highly mineralized; suitable land is often red or black. This may upset your VLF detector. Be certain that your machine has a manual adjustment of the ground effect to compensate for this intense mineralization. Also favor a high-frequency detector (14, 18kHz, or more) which are very efficient on small nugget type targets and much better in mineralized ground. A pulse induction (PI) detector will be almost insensitive to mineralization, which is why they are very popular for gold research even if they are almost unable to reject metals (they only work in all mode metals).

Gold recovery tools

Gold panning and another good method of finding native gold, a hobby, a passion, or a profession for certain.

The basics of gold panning:

The practice is simple and I invite you to discover the technique to search for gold. Depending on your budget or your time for this activity, several methods can be used end to end for maximum performance. You will have to train on the technique of locating the best corner to find gold. The rivers and their alluviums, the torrents and their pots or crevices (fault in the rock), the beds are the river beds after a flood. But it will also require you to do a whole new technical vocabulary with the use of a Pan, or a Battée or even a Sluice

This method of looking for gold is particularly engaging. When the time comes to separate the gold flakes from the last grains of black sand after sieving and then breeding, the pleasure is very intense. And just like in metal detection, certain regions are to be favored for gold panning. The Paris region is less favorable than Gard or Ariège. But it is not necessary to go far from home to take your first steps in this activity and to be able to find gold.

Selection of the best gold panning kits:

- Complete Garrett gold panning set

- Batée 36cm

- Pitch 25.4cm or Pitch 25cm

- Complete beginner's gold panning set

- Beginner sluice for gold panning or Compact Sluice box for gold panning

Our selection of basic material for gold panning is the minimum necessary to practice as part of a hobby. Requiring a small budget, these kits are ready to use and upgradeable. Younger children, novices, or even those who are already gold miners will manage to find native gold if patience and technique are available.

Like metal detection, this activity is normally subject to prefectural authorization so as not to change the nature of the rivers and therefore the flora and fauna found there. This authorization also allows you to know that you have to plug the holes and that you should not use a backhoe or excavator type machine otherwise this is similar to a professional activity.

It is within everyone's reach to find gold. But still, it takes a little practice to achieve its ends. If you have free time and a little patience, you can probably acquire it without taking out the credit card. You still need to invest in a VLF detector or a pulsed induction detector, or even gold panning equipment. Once the purchase is made, all that remains is to find the right place to find gold in the form of a nugget, a coin, or glitter.

Chapter Seven

Your first finds

On starting your detection, your detector beeped, you have pinpointed the area and you are ready to dig. Do not dig directly at the target but start at the side while approaching slowly. Use pinpoint to make sure you are still in the right direction. The detector determines the depth so dig accordingly.

Once the target is located, go out there, examine it visually by brushing it lightly. If it's interesting, put it in a freezer pocket and write down where you found it. It is not uncommon for an old purse full of coins to fall to the ground and disseminate targets over a large area around it. Also, note it on your little logbook.

Once dug up, fill the hole to leave no traces, you have to respect nature and places! I insist on this point because, for the detectorists to be respected, it is up to us to respect the excavation sites.

How to transport your finds?

So let's talk about what you should do with your finds to protect them during the rest of your metal hunt. If you remember the code of ethics for metal detection, we will also dispose of waste responsibly during our detections. There is a good chance that you would have a lot of waste. That's why you need a belt pouch or a bum bag that has at least two pockets - one for your bargains and one for your trash cans. This facilitates the selection of waste at the end of your hunt. And if you find something very interesting like a coin or a piece of jewelry, you probably won't want to throw it away with the rest of your finds at the risk of damaging it. What I recommend is that you also carry with you (usually in your carrying bag, not your pocket) a special plastic case stuffed with cotton balls.

What to do with found items

Every good detector respects the finds and the objects he finds. If your object has an interest that may interest history, art, or archeology, we advise you to contact a competent person. Don't deprive the world of your finds. Unfortunately, 95% of excavators keep the finds for themselves, for fear of problems with the law or simply for their collection.

It's up to you to act and act according to your conscience, but if you decide to keep the targets, as the coins, for example, treat them carefully or give them away. If you search to put your finds in the dustbin, don't do detection.

Cleaning your finds

The first thing to know is simply that you need to know what your finds can be worth. Why? Simply because you could ruin your room by cleaning it if you want to resell it (or even keep it). You can wear a soft bristle toothbrush in your pocket so that you can do a light cleaning in the field when you have trouble identifying a find.

In terms of cleaning when you are back home, you will need to stick with a soft-bristle toothbrush, warm water, and dish soap. Avoid harsh chemicals as they can eat away at the metal. For seriously rusted relics, many people opt for a procedure called electrolysis. Another way people clean their finds (especially low-value items) is by using a stone cup.

Never clean any of your finds if you are unsure of their value, and there is even the slightest possibility that you may wish to sell it. This could seriously ruin its value, especially for rare coins.

Chapter Eight

Frequently Asked Questions

Q: Why sometimes the depth of the instrument is not reached during detection?

A: The detection depth of all instruments depends very much on the surface, shape, and weight of the metal. In general, the larger the area, the higher the number and the greater the depth of detection. Conversely, the smaller the area, the smaller the number and the smaller the corresponding depth. The depth of the instrument is the maximum depth that can be reached in the best conditions, following the industrial standards of the product. The depth of detection will vary depending on the quality of the soil. For example, if the soil is wet or the density is high, the signal strength of the metal will be weakened and the detection depth of the metal detector. Moreover, the detection depth is also reduced in the event of low power and insufficient transmission power. In this case, please replace the battery in time.

Q: How do you get the best detection results?

A: The detection effect is improved when the ground is dry or the metal is buried for a long time.

The more the metal is buried, the deeper the detection depth. Since the metal buried in the ground for a long time will be gradually oxidized to produce metallic rust, distributed around and the surrounding soil reacts to produce an intense magnetic field on the metal surface increases, also increases the signal strength. The longer the time, the greater the signal strength and the depth of detection!

Q: What should I watch out for when servicing underground metal detectors?

A: Do not probe in the rain as most buried metal detectors are not waterproof. If the panel gets into water, it may cause short circuits or other faults. Remove the battery when not in use, as the battery can be corroded and corroded by the card for a long time. Store it in a dry place when not in use for a long time.

Q: How deep can underground metal detectors be?

A: The depth of detection of the detector is related to the metallic material and the shape of the detected object and the quality of the ground of the detected object. The depth of detection of the same detector in different regions is completely different.

In the air (i.e. floating), the depth of detection of the underground metal detector is not detected. When the instrument and the earth have a magnetic induction balance, the best detection effect is achieved: if it is suspended in the air, the magnetic induction balance cannot be reached! For example, if a silver element can be detected at a distance of 20 cm, if the silver element is buried in the ground, the depth of detection will increase considerably, and the longer it will be buried, the easier it will be to detect. Since the metal buried in the ground for a long time will be gradually oxidized to produce metallic rust, distributed around and the surrounding soil reacts to produce an intense magnetic field on the metal surface increases, also increases the signal strength.

Q: Are there places where detection is prohibited?

This is a frequently asked question. Leisure detection is framed by law. And this one is very clear. As long as your detection is not for an archaeological purpose, you can buy and use a metal detector. There are places where detection is prohibited. These include, for example, the site of the Battle of Verdun, the Normandy landing beaches, or certain beaches such as Deauville or

Trouville. Here you will find the ranges where you cannot use your metal detector.

Q: Is a helmet necessary for metal detection?

Many people are hesitant to buy headphones and beginners are wondering what they can be used for. The helmet can be useful to you. It already allows you not to disturb the people around you. It can also be practical if the environment is noisy and will give you a better perception of sounds since they will go directly into your ears!

Q: Is metal detection dangerous for health?

If you think about the electromagnetic currents that are emitted by your metal detector, no they are not dangerous for your health. For the rest, there are of course precautions to be taken during your detective trips. Pay attention, for example, to your back with the correct posture. Also watch out for sunburn, sunstroke (sunscreen and cap obligatory), tetanus (check your vaccines), ticks (wear high shoes), and insects (always have a repellent with you).

About the Author

Frederick Coble grew up in Nye County in Gold rich Nevada in a family of treasure hunters. He became interested in treasure hunting and gold prospecting at the age of 14, hunting for the precious metal in several Gold Districts alongside his father's metal detector. This interest got him to carry out several types of research on how to study historical maps and prospect for lost treasures and precious metals. Fredrick purchased his first metal detector (Gold Bug) in 1994 and his expeditions have yielded so much finds (gold nuggets, precious metals, historical coins and other relics) running into millions of dollars in sales. One of his accomplished finds is a 50kg gold nugget in 2010.

Frederick still lives in Nye County with his wife and two beautiful daughters.